Carlos

A Tail OF SURVIVAL

Written By **Dr. Blanc Cooper and wife, Debby**

CARLOS

"Carlos" is a true story witnessed and written
by Dr. Blane Cooper, DVM and spouse Debby Cooper;
whose lives have been spent caring for animals.

This storybook is dedicated to all those
who love animals as much as they do.

Found at Walmart

My first memory-warm, safe,
and full of mother's milk.

LIFE IS GOOD.

What could be better?

Then, *"What Happened?"*

Hot Hot Hot
Hungry Hungry Hungry
Can't see...
"Help me Someone"
Two Angels appeared.
I could hear their voices;
they were there
to rescue me.

"Oh my, it's a tiny kitten."

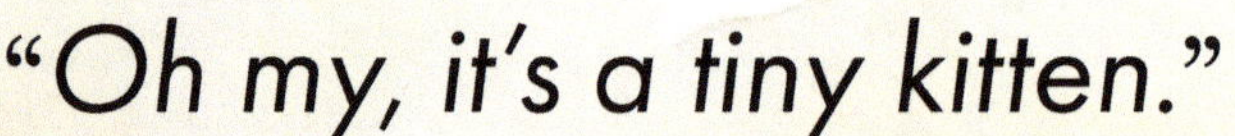

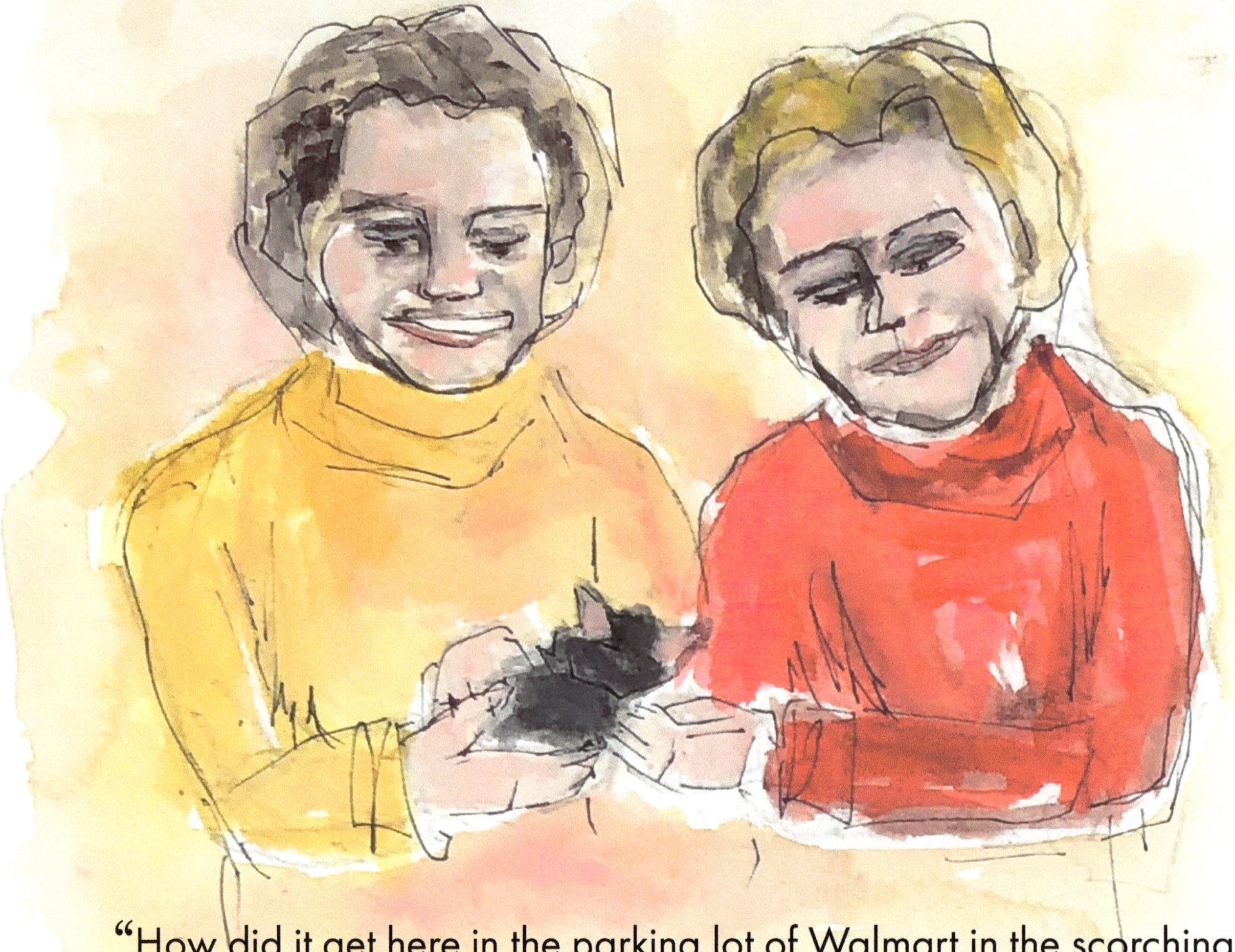

"How did it get here in the parking lot of Walmart in the scorching sun?
It can't walk and it's eyes aren't open yet."

"We must do something."

What a day!

A New Family!

Well, the Angels took me immediately to their veterinarian and pleaded with him
to please help me. I couldn't breathe and felt weak, hot, and sleepy.
Dr. C immediately cooled me off with cool water and a fan.
I started feeling better soon, but, was very hungry.

Dr. C gave me some liquid which kind of
    tasted like mother's milk.

        Just not quite as tasty. It was good though.

Dr. C talked to me, fed me, swaddled me,
and loved me back to my old self.
Soon, I opened my eyes and couldn't
believe all there was to see.

Another cat who might be my mother?

No, she said she wasn't.

Her name was Betsy Johnson
and she was very pretty
and friendly.

Then, there was this big blue dog
(Maria). She didn't seem to care
for me much. She was curious though.

And, the most unusual new addition
to my life was this big green and yellow
bird (Ricky). He seemed to like me and
he was talking to me. Telling me Hello
and all kinds of crazy things.

Dr. C and his wife really took good care of me
and all of the family seemed to love me.
I was content with my new family.

Seeing the World

Even though Dr. C was still feeding me a bottle,
I was able to go places I had never ever
expected to be able to go.
My first out of town trip was to the
beautiful Mississippi Gulf Coast.

I got to ride in an elevator and spend the night
in a luxurious room with a couch,
table to play under
and a view of the ocean.

It was kitty heaven.

Next, I actually went to Florida. A purrfect kitten vacation spot.
There were children to play with, curtains to hide in and I loved
riding on the dash of the car on the way.
And, I found a great sleeping place, an open suitcase.

I had so much fun.

Then, I went to Arkansas to visit Dr. C's daughter
and she had more friends for me
Two big dogs, 3 nice cats and a big
deck to look out over.

How could I be so lucky to
end up where I am?

Fate, I guess.

Home at Last

As I grew, I started liking milk less and crunchy cat food better.
I liked the sound it made when I ate it. Yum.
I still missed my milk a little. But, it just didn't fill me up.

I was allowed to stay at home by myself also.
I could do anything I wanted all day long.

Ricky, Betsy Johnson, and I napped
most of the day and were
ready when Dr. C, his wife and the big
blue dog, Maria, came home.

We couldn't wait to play with
them, listen to their reports of the day
and get ready to sleep some more later on.

They were kind enough to let me sleep in the bed with them.

They also let me go outside to look at
wild birds, turtles,
squirrels, chipmunks, and snakes.
There was so much to see and do,
I didn't know where to begin or stop.

Exhausting for sure.

Happy Happy Happy

I continue to enjoy my
wonderful life with my found family.

I feel like the luckiest cat
in the world.
I have everything a feline
would wish for.

Food, Water, Litter,
and a loving
extended family.

All is well. And that's the truth.

THE TAIL END

About the Author

Dr. Blane Cooper and wife Debby have owned and operated Cooper Animal Hospital for over 45 years. Though the years, they have strived to give the best care and compassion to all who come their way. As strong supporters of the Leflore County Humane Society and Southern Mutts Rescue, they aid in adopting countless homeless pets. As they continue their journey through life, they will continue doing their best to care for all God's creatures.

ISBN 979-8-218-07806-5

www.ingramcontent.com/pod-product-compliance
Lightning Source LLC
Chambersburg PA
CBHW042020110726
48006CB00004B/1162